This
Book
Belongs
To _____

Book Club Edition

The Story of Samson

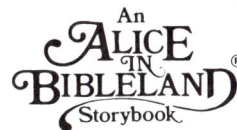

Written by Alice Joyce Davidson
Illustrated by Victoria Marshall

Text copyright © 1997 by Alice Joyce Davidson
Art copyright © 1997 by The C.R. Gibson Company
Published by The C.R. Gibson Company
Norwalk, Connecticut 06856
Printed in the United States of America
All rights reserved.
ISBN 0-7667-1732-1

A little girl named Alice
Liked to exercise and run.
She tumbled and she rode her bike,
And jumped rope just for fun.

And when she wanted to relax,
She'd curl up in her nook,
And read a favorite part
Of her Bible storybook.

Alice read of Samson
And how God had made him strong.
Then the airmail bird flew up to her
And brought this note along:
"Reading is the magic key
To take you where you want to be."

Her storybook became a screen.
The screen grew tall and wide,
Then Alice took a little walk
To Bibleland inside.

She saw a woman listening
To an angel God had sent.
He said, "You'll have a baby soon,
A truly blessed event."

"Your baby boy will grow up strong,
And follow in God's way,
And he will help save Israel
From the Philistines one day.

"You'll find your son is different
From children everywhere,
And one thing you must never do
Is cut your baby's hair."

She named her baby, Samson.
What the angel said was true.
He was not like other children,
He was fearless—stronger, too.

As Samson grew to be a man,
His hair was thick and long.
He knew to never cut it,
For his hair had made him strong.

He saw many Philistines.
He often fought them, too.
For the Philistines were wicked,
And evil through and through.

Samson had adventures
That proved his strength and might,
And he soon became the leader
Of the other Israelites.

The Philistines knew of his strength
And feared this mighty man.
They wanted to destroy him,
So they came up with this plan.

The Philistines had told her,
"We must know before too long
Where Samson gets his power.
Is it God who makes him strong?"

"What's the secret of your strength?"
She questioned him each day.
He said, "Tie me up with bowstrings,
And my strength will fade away."

While Samson slept, she tied his arms
With bowstrings that were new.
When Samson woke, he laughed, then
Broke them all in two.

Delilah kept on asking him,
"How did you get so strong?"
And Samson kept on teasing her
With answers that were wrong.

Delilah had his secret,
And with the greatest care,
The next time Samson fell asleep,
She quickly cut his hair.

When Samson woke, his strength was gone.
He had no strength to fight,
And the Philistines imprisoned him
And blinded him that night.

He was forced to push a millstone
Like an animal each day.
He was teased and treated badly
By all who came his way.

One day at a festival
They thought it would be fun
To bring Samson to the temple
To be teased by everyone.

The temple was completely filled
With Philistines everywhere.
The Israelites saw that Samson
Once more had grown long hair.

Samson found some pillars,
Then he prayed to God above
To help him save his people,
Then he gave a mighty shove.

The roof fell on the Philistines
And all the people scattered.
Samson saved the Israelites
And that was all that mattered.

The time had come for Alice
To leave that Bible scene.
She thought of all the things she learned
As she walked right through her screen.

"God had chosen Samson
To free the Israelites.
He gave him strength and courage
To fight for what is right.

"Though Samson told his secret
And his strength did go away,
God restored him once again
So he could save the day.